## RAINSHADOW EDITIONS

Garnet Moon. Paul Zarzyski. 1990.

Seven Nevada Poets. Ed. William L. Fox. 1991.

With Respect for Distance. Gailmarie Pahmeier. 1992.

Generous Journeys/Travesias Generosas. Marjorie Agosín. 1992.

Snowmelt. Shaun T. Griffin. 1994.

Geograph. William L. Fox. 1994.

Furniture Dreams. Marjorie Agosín. 1995.

Ride the Silence. Linda Hussa. 1995.

The Rings Around Saturn. Maria Theresa Maggi. 1996.

The Concept of Bodily Objects. Catherine Webster. 1997.

Bones Set Against the Drift. Bill Cowee. 1998.

And I You. Donna Hanelin. 1998.

Nothing We Lose Can Be Replaced. Tom Meschery. 1999.

# NOTHING WE LOSE

## CAN BE REPLACED

POEMS BY **Tom Meschery**

Rainshadow Editions · The Black Rock Press
University of Nevada, Reno · 1999

Printed in the United States of America

ISBN  1-891033-15-8

Rainshadow Editions
The Black Rock Press
University Library/322
University of Nevada, Reno
Reno, NV 89557-0044

Previous appearances:

"Four Letters from Nicholai Tolstoy ... "
"Student Returns to Reno High to Visit"
Published in *Barnabe Mountain Review,* #4.


Cover: St. Basil's Cathedral in Moscow

# Acknowledgments

My thanks to Jim Whitehead and Gary Short for their
first careful read, and especially to Morton Marcus whose
loving criticism, precise suggestions, and editing made
this book possible.

*For Joanne, Janai, Megan, and Matthew*

# Contents

## Teaching

## Dying in Russia

"Stately mansions, gardens pretty,
Churches tall with domes of gold,
Fair and wondrous to behold."

*Alexander Pushkin*

## A Small Embrace

*Maria Vladimirovna Lvov   1903 - 1989*

In Siberia the snow grows from the ground,
trees of snow, grass of snow, white wheat,
the coldest rye. Three thousand miles of snow,
a few villages, some bony dogs, peasants
out to wave the last of us goodbye. Each day
our train plowed through those white fields,
Aunt Moussia said we left behind a crop of crosses,
"enough to satisfy the appetite of any Bolshevik."

Coal stoves centered in each car
rocked back and forth like drunkards.
All we burned was wood, wet and green
that smoked so much we kept the windows open.
Cold stuck anything we touched;
even within our gloves skin froze.
And beards. Hair fell like icicles
to the floor and did not melt.

We knelt on the shores of Lake Baikal
and pressed our faces against ice to see
a dying species, ancient fish we'd read about
as children, trapped below the surface, scales
magnified as clear as fingernails. Aboard the train
missionaries, thinking we were praying
to something heathen in the lake, threatened us
with forests filled with Trotsky's partisans.

No one ever smiled enough that I remember.
Your grandmother gave it up for good.
Your grandfather's last letter, postmarked
Paris, said God had called him back to Russia.
I couldn't think of anything except
the miles and miles of snow on snow

our train was cutting through like scissors,
land like a sheet of white paper falling off
behind us on either side of the tracks, our lost lives.

Too young, my brothers had filled
their pockets with their only history:
marbles, colored pencils, tin soldiers,
dreams no bigger than trinkets.

But I had already kissed a boy
and left him behind to kiss other girls
or to die kissing the cold ground.
Do you understand how such a small
embrace can be like a country?

Tom, nothing we lose can be replaced.
The further from our homes we fled,
the more we lived through photographs:
starch in our white summer dresses,
our croquet set, why Misha wore
his sailor's hat cocked so aslant,
the great hall chandelier, the Afgan rug
in papa's study, embroidery on mother's pillows,
the way our icons shone in the corners
of our rooms above their candles.

My father said our icons were like family.
Still, we couldn't save them all, only the holiest
sewn into linings of our clothes—
the smallest, our Blessed Lady of Iversk,
in my brassiere, close to my heart.
Svetapolk and Svetaslav, the boy saints,
in the hem of my skirt. Each time
we moved we were a moving church.

In Harbin, safe at last, we made our homes or tried.
There was no work. To live, we pried the jewels,
one by one, from the halos of our Saints
for rent, warm coats, shoes that never seemed
to keep the northern Chinese weather out.
Next, we sold the saints themselves,
like slaves. Their gold brought just enough
to see us through one year. Poor nobility,
how we suffered, untrained for anything.
It wasn't long before I saw counts drunk,
countesses leaving for brothels in Shanghai.
Some nights our young men, bored and full of vodka,
slipped back into Siberia to fight the Reds
as if dying was the only job they could find.

I wept because two breasts were not enough
to comfort all of them. One soldier, no older
than you are now, screamed he was a bird
and flew through glass. The broken shards
on the sidewalk looked like feathers in the sun.

Your father was one of those young men.
We married quickly, out of mutual kindness.
For most of us, all that was left of passion was survival.

The day he left, the ocean widening between our waves,
he yelled his promise from the ship, to make a home,
then send for us. I knew it would be more than years.
We women understand the old story of departure. His letter of
December, '41, came a month too late for anything but war.

The first year in the concentration camp
you broke your collar bone. Outside the hospital window
the cherry trees were blooming. First, we heard
the Japanese were winning. Then, the Americans.
We were never treated cruelly. The Red Cross parachutes

with packages of food and clothing fell like mercy.
When the atom bomb fell, we were already bombed out
in Tokyo, walking the streets, sleeping in the rubble.
I carried you on my back. Your sister was too heavy.

Remember this photograph: these clothes
the army gave us, called fatigues, that never fit,
no matter how I tucked and sewed. The letters D.P.
stenciled on our sleeves, they made us wear,
seemed so shameful. Tom, I didn't need to be reminded.
I knew the minute I left Russia when I was nineteen,
no matter where I lived, I'd always be displaced.
At last in San Francisco, walking down the gangplank
into crowds waving family names above their heads,
a voice kept yelling over a loudspeaker: citizens to the left,
stateless to the right. A band was playing something cheerful.
You pointed to the wrong father. I to the wrong husband.

## Russian Center

In the Russian Center on Sutter Street
no one has died. The Tsar is still alive,
so is the Tsarina, and all her sweet children.
The Grand Duke Nicholas survived
And there is the Baroness, splendid as always
in the latest styles from Paris. While Anna
Vyrubova still looks like a seamstress
in the photograph three frames down
from Count Yusoupov who helped kill
Rasputin, a Saint too vile even for Russia.
Here, those old scandals are never too late.
Sonya Andreevna and the young count,
what's his name, caught fucking
in that same closet, as if it were yesterday
and the revolution never happened.

## Aunts

Irina Ivanovna complains, her voice
gone slightly tipsy: *The Revolution
was a dreadful mistake.* Given the choice,
who would have left? Who leaves
a dinner with a full plate,
a full glass still on the table?

The other aunt swears she'd shovel shit
first before she'd join those San Francisco
nouveux riche, so called blue bloods
from Pacific Heights. Irina Ivanovna
sews her title, Princess, into clothes
and makes good money from women
dying for nobility. Neither aunt knows
or cares that I am wide awake, my bedroom
door ajar, listening to the life we lost:
the grand ballroom in St. Petersburg,
our estates they spent their girlhood summers in,
autumn trips to Paris. They scold my mother
for her unbeluga tins, champagne unfit to drink,
day old bread, missing crystal. *Oh, caviar,*
the princess weeps for elegance.

*We were not Cinderellas,
for pity's sake.
Why run from our own fairytale?*

Imperial Russia, no farther than ear-shot
of my bedroom. One aunt says she's had enough.
The other says Tsar Nicholas, the weakling,
and his German wife spoiled everything.
A rush for coats, kisses cheek to cheek.

All the way to the door, Irina Ivanova argues
they should join high society, those commoners,
even if they were beneath their station,
were the closest thing to Russia in America.

## Russian Easter

Incense, and all those San Francisco saints
on their knees, some rising, some standing,
erect and holy. From the choir overhead,
my father's reluctant bass chants:
Господи Господи помилуй
My mother's fingers sign the trinity across herself,
shoulder to shoulder, forehead to floor.
These broad and sweeping flourishes
touch only the air around her body:
*A woman bears her body like a cross*
*from womb to birth*—my thirteen pound breech,
and all such deliveries from evil. Oh, Lord,
deliver me from such holiness or soon I'll join
the prone supplicants, the kneeling babushkas.
At last outside, when we light candles
from flames rising from our cupped hands,
and follow the procession three times
circling the church, Mother of God,
we will enter as we always have into your body
of Christ, father and I, as we did tonight
and all those Easter Sundays together, ever after.

## Four Letters from Nicholai Tolstoy from the Austrian Front to his Cousin, Maria Vladimirovna Lvov

September 2, 1914

Arrived on furlough just in time
to attend the ball Countess Kleimichel gave
for the beau monde of St. Petersburg.
Ladies with hair dyed blue waltzed
with half naked cavemen. What buffoons.
Sadly, I saw Princess Xenia Alexandrovna
among them with her beautiful
daughter. Later, women dressed
as fish swam on the floor
over yards of blue satin while men
with fishnets tried to catch them.

Ma chere cousine, this war
has turned us into minnows.
Remember Lieutenant Cherniavsky
of the Preobrajensky Guards?
Only three days before, I saw
an Austrian officer run past him
as he lay wounded on the ground
and fire a bullet into his neck.

September 13, 1914

Tomorrow, I'm told we'll try
to cross the river San. Our losses will be great.
The Austrians have dug their trenches,
and only bayonets will carry the day.
I know I'm going to die.
Our poor peasant soldiers shake their heads
and make the sign of the cross
from shoulder to shoulder
so slowly that by the time they finish
battles could be won or lost.
I must close because it is getting dark
and I have no candle.


October 29, 1914

Ma chere cousine, imagine I'm running,
waving my saber above my head
setting a good example for my troops.
I keep looking back and yelling at them
to keep up. To my right, a cavalry charge.
I'm happy I didn't join the cavalry.
They have so much farther to fall before they die.
What did Faustus say, "O lente, lente currite noctis equi"
just as he was about to lose his soul?
The horses are perfectly trained, charging on
even without their riders. One horse,
bless him, has destroyed a machine gun
all by himself. As I run toward the crazed beast
I see he is killing the same man more than twice.

February 20, 1915

We won the battle. General Brusilov himself
thanked me. He never once mentioned the blood
on my forehead. Trop politesse. My men cheered
as he pinned the St. George Cross on my chest.
Papa will be delighted. After the ceremony
I found Captain Markov and Lieutenant Gargarin,
you remember the young Prince? I laid down beside
them and pulled their bodies over me like blankets.

## Mashtakov, the Cossack

Each month he took our rent,
he left behind Paris movie sets —
1920's cabarets owned by emigré
ex-colonels of the Imperial Guard,
Hollywood's favorite Russian script.
He liked saying he was the star
while the maitre-de, a Romanoff
Prince, and waitress countess
so and so, were merely extras,
expendable - plenty of nobility
out of work, just waiting
for the chance to play themselves.
He'd danced with bears
eaten glass and slapped his heels
enough years to become rich,
buy six apartments he rented
only to the upper class: the old
general always a week behind
and the Baroness who fucked him
on account. After he left
Mother complained no doubt
he'd be a peasant to the day
he died. Father called him a гуран,
a tartar. Monthly at the same time
he'd ride out of the Asian steppes
to put the Boyars in their place,
demanding cash. Never checks.

# Letter from Saint Petersburg

*For Max Crawford*

Militsa, I am reading a letter
dated 1917, written by our grandfather,
Senator Lvov, to his wife
because a friend called asking me for help
collecting facts for his book.
about the Revolution to be called *Red and White*.

It will say plenty about survival
under dreadful conditions.

Our grandfather is complaining
all the best families
are leaving Russia. *Every day
another door opens
and closes*. His exact words.

*Soon there will be no one*.
Outside, he says the workers
are warming their hands
over blazing furniture,
and *icons are going up in smoke*.

## The Cadets

*The Graduating Class of the Imperial Academy*


The best way to remember them—they are young
and full of horseplay, staring into the mouths of cannons,
wrestling, waving sabers, or posing, arms across their chests,
trying to look too serious to be taken seriously.
One cadet always seems cross-eyed or on the verge of laughing.
And, sometimes, at the edge of battle, soldiers marching
in the background, an officer is taking a piss,
grinning like a school boy at the camera.

In some photographs they are riding horses.
In the saddle they seem graceful and at ease as if at home
where certain manners are expected.
One stands in his stirrups, doffs his hat and bows.
Another blows a kiss. Against the black pages of the album,
their first names and patronymics, months and years
stand out in white ink below each picture.
If killed, the place and how they died is also written,
*Sergei Mihailovich, March, 1918, Tomsk. Thrown from his horse.*
On the next page, his brother, *Andre Mihailovich,*
*December, 1919, bullet wounds to the chest.*

In San Francisco, the survivors formed a club they called Cadets.
Each month, at the Russian Center, they held a meeting
to toast one another and anniversaries of old battles,
the birthdays of all the Tsars with vodka. I met them once,
the only time I saw my father drunk. The next time I saw them
together, at my father's funeral, they had grown too old
to be Cadets, in my mind a name for highjinks, playfulness.
Today, who knows how many are alive.
Their photographs are better than their ghosts.

# My Mother's Diaries — A History of Non-Sequiturs

*"...no one turning over our letters has*
  *yet understood how completely and*
*how deeply faithless we are, which is*
  *to say: how true we are to ourselves.*

  Marina Tsvetayeva

*For Vladimir Nikolaevich Lvov, my grandfather.*


Vladimir Nikolaevich, newly elected Ober-Procurator,
lives at 34 Liteinaya Street, former home of Grishka Rasputin,
that dreadful monk. The Ober-Procurator's wife
can not bear the sinfulness. She asks a priest to come
and bless each room before the furniture arrives,
before she hangs one painting on the wall.

* * *

Breshko-Breshkovskaya, babushka, grandmother
of the revolution and the Ober-Procurator meet
on a train to Moscow. What did they say
to one another? I can only imagine—his privilege,
her years in exile in Siberia. Her voice they said
was like a sailor's, was more like a sparrow's.
She could have answered, it snowed
for twenty days and nights in a row, sometimes
into the barracks through the broken windows,
but the clarity, the clarity of winter light—aristocrats
will never understand. The Ober-Procurator
would have been polite, though quizzical.

* * *

The Ober-Procurator believes Kerensky is the man
to save Russia. The Ober-Procurator's wife says
there is no hope for him if he remains an atheist.

* * *

In Petrograd, massive demonstrations along the Nevsky Prospect
and the Fields of Marovo. Silly Anyuta, putting on lipstick
because the soldiers are so handsome rushes into the street
and is nearly trampled. The Ober-Procurator saves her
and returns home with a headache. Fools shooting into the air.
Signs saying: *Down with the Duma and the Council.*

* * *

Bogarouslan, March 1917. Red flags in the cathedral square.
A soldier making a speech about freedom, knowledge, and labor.
Another soldier standing on the top of the church waving his cap.
"We are free," he yells and jumps unhurt into the snow.
Two women whispering, it's safer to be against the old regime
otherwise they might be killed or poisoned. Riots and arson
in Bugulma, Aunt Mousia writes their peasants used pitchforks:
*the love-seat, Mashinka, the one you like so much torn to shreds.*

The Ober-Procurator takes tea with Kerensky, the social democrat,
newly elected President of the Provisional Government, to discuss
the Tsar imprisoned, the fate of the Russian church. The Ober-Procurator
swears, after him no more ober-procurators; he will sign the document,
return the church to the church and the people. There is no written proof
anywhere of this meeting in history, except this: *The toast was hard,
the marmalade we ate came from England. Kerensky, a slight man,
almost feminine, may not be strong enough to bear this burden.*

* * *

Krotkovo, Lvov's estates. You walk to the river with your watercolors
and your diary: *Misha, shot for no reason by an anarchist.
All the maids are attending a meeting of free women.* Before sunset,
the light is perfect. In the margins, you have painted miniatures
of birches, first flowering crocus, ice breaking, purple shadows.

* * *

Anna Petrovna writes from the capital she dined with the Protopopovs.
The dinner was unsettling; machine guns firing from the streets.
They drank the last of the French chablis and talked of Finland.

* * *

Your mother writes: *Father finally returned from the Troitsky-Sergiev*
*Monastary. All the monks agreed with him Meropolit Makary*
*had to go. Rumors the Ober-Procurator threatened the old priest*
*with a pistol until he promised to resign. Ridiculous. I blame Kerensky*
*for these rumors. You know your father never owned a pistol.*

* * *

Petrograd is unpresentable. Trash scattered everywhere.
The streets so dusty, people hardly breathe. Alexei Nikitich says
they are all rascals. First they force the Tsar to abdicate and now
they dare to hang the paintings at the Tretiakovsky in the wrong light.

* * *

The Emperor and his family are abandoned and forgotten.

* * *

Alexandrovsky Palace, Tsarskoi-Selo. Princess Anastasia,
wearing a white dress, runs into the garden.
"What will happen to us if the Bolsheviks triumph,"
she asks the young guard. The guard answers,
"You will all be spared except your German mother.
She will probably be hung." The Princess bursts into tears.
The young guard trys to console her. He might have succeeded
except you write: *He dared to touch her shoulder.*

* * *

During the revolution angels appear in the towns and cities
all over Russia. They hold out their hands wounded like Christ's.
The people mistake them for beggars and toss them coins.
The Bolsheviks say they are symbolic. Somebody writes:
*History is unreliable. August is undisputed.*

* * *

More than once your diary says the Ober-Procurator
saved the Russian Church and should be canonized.
Saint, grandfather. Kerensky was not so kind in his history:
*Mostly, Lvov was a fool and naive. He and Kornilov,*
*an even greater fool, plotting against my government.*
*I telegraphed the general, said I was Lvov and discovered*
*everything.* This is part of history. This is not:
Before he met Kornilov at the hotel in Mogilev
and later Kerensky at the Winter Palace,
the Ober-Procurator suffered terrible headaches.

* * *

The Ober-Procurator can not sleep. In the next room
Kerensky walks back and forth, back and forth
bellowing arias from Rigoletto, La Dona Mobile,
Nessun Dorma from Turandot. The Ober-Procurator,
bewildered, tries to understand the sequence of events
leading to his arrest. Dawn comes just in time.
For what? Some questions about his sanity. Psychiatrists
measuring the size of his skull. They give him laxatives.

* * *

Winter Palace. The Ober-Procurater bribes the guards and leaves
by the garden gate. He wears his top coat and carries his umbrella.
The train to Orenburg is on a time. He shaves his beard.
He lives in hiding with the son of Nikolai Tolstoy, born out of wedlock,
named Malenkov. I like the part about the bodies best.
The wounds, he said, are roses. Grandfather of metaphors,
a man Nobokov *pere* calls completely untrustworthy.

* * *

Your diary says Tsar Nicholas the Second wept for the Ober-Procurator.

German Zeppelins threating Petrograd. Kerensky hears Lvov
and Kornilov have escaped. As usual, when confronted with bad news,
Kerensky faints. Some say this is a ploy. Others say he is delicate.
Lenin and the Bolsheviks sense weakness and gain the upper hand.
Uncle Lyosha and Aunt Mousia pray for a Napoleon.

* * *

The Russian Revolution is filled with shadowy figures, meddlers,
traitors, ignoramuses, collaborators, liars, hooligans,
side by side with visionaries, demons, saints, martyrs, patriots.
Always there are words like episodes, collusions, conspiracies.
*Suspicions that the whole Kornilov Affair was a provocation.*
Exhausted and feeling used, The Ober-Procurator disappears.
Two years without a word. Kolchak's western front collapses.

* * *

When you write,"we left Russia for good in 1920",
Vladimir Nikolaevich suddenly appears in France, a continent
away from China and you. He publishes a literary magazine
for Russian emigrés. Within four years he will have a new wife,
you know nothing about—until much later a letter arrives
from Paris, the Tolstoys gossiping. *Dear Mashinka,
your saintly father, the bigamist, plans to return to Russia
and take his peasant woman, already pregnant, with him.*

* * *

San Francisco, 1948.  At ten, I believe you when you whisper
the Ober-Procurator is still alive in the Soviet Union
under an assumed name, working secretly for the Tsar's return.
One finger on my lips, swearing me to silence.

\* \* \*

The police report says my father and his Cadet pals,
drunk and disorderly, drive their car into a wall
near Stanford University where Kerinsky is lecturing
on his life among the Bolsheviks. In the trunk
the police find one loaded pistol, two swords
and a photograph of Tsar Nicholas the Second.

\* \* \*

The husband of the daughter of the Ober-Procurator
spends the night in jail, or so the family story goes,
singing Russian hymns and swearing vengence
on that social democrat. When I ask you why,
all you give me is a history of my father's voice,
a basso profundo, strong enough to sing in operas.

\* \* \*

Kerensky writes his memoir, dismissing the Ober-Procurator
as a meddler. Nekrasov, *Kerensky's eminence grise,*
*a thoroughly sinister figure,* thinks otherwise: *V.N. Lvov*
*helped save the Revolution by exposing Kornilov.*
Before his suicide, Kornilov tries to imagine what went wrong.
He blames the Ober-Procurator's height, almost seven feet.
*I would have known a mystic from a simpleton if only*
*I could have looked him straight in the eyes.*

\* \* \*

Kerensky dies in his sleep. You tell me that by morning
you'll be gone, back to Russia to assist your saintly father.
All night I listen for the door to close.

\* \* \*

You say the Ober-Procurator lived to ninety and died in Omsk.
You have no proof of this. Later, in a footnote, I read: *Some say*
*Vladimir Nikolaevich Lvov, Ober-Procurator*
*of the Holy Synod, ended his days as a derelict on the streets of Paris.*

# With My Sister Looking At Our Family Tree

Suddenly, we discover generations,
dangling like hung corpses. So many,
this moment might be a scene
in a western movie starring
a hanging judge gone beserk,
the paper flat as a prairie
and just as brown with age,
filled with scaffolds.
For this split second, two
Tolstoy brothers stand apart
waiting to drop, hurtle into history
to father famous writers.

When I tell you this, you laugh,
accusing me of cultural confusion,
what I get for being too American.
*There is no hanging tradition*
*in Russia, except some notable*
*suicides.* Sergei Esenin comes to mind
and a less poetic uncle who swindled
the bank he worked for out of millions.

I say our family tree is heavy
with great men, the names
you count so much on. Outside,
the wind through cottonwoods
is blowing leaves across the window.
We're in the West all right.
If we're not careful, the weight
of family pride, like trap doors,
will wrench from under us,
and the branch we're hanging on will break.

## Bedside Conversation (After a watercolor by Столица)

A black-robed, full-bearded priest
waving crosses over me, his breath
so garlic I will see that field

filled with Russian peasants,
his bedside prayers so mournful
they will force me back to old beliefs.

Unreligioned, this would be my choice,
to die Orthodox, for whatever it's worth.
I'll take my chances with my parents' grace.

## Language Barrier

Father, when you speak English
it's like a man losing his breath,
your hands always trying to make sure.
Clenched fist means anger.
Thumb up, approval.
In confusion, your fingers
groping in the space between us.
Some signs I never learn.

When your voice fails,
you return to Russian.
But I turn away.
Foreigners, we live together
with no common language.

## The Game Was Ours

" ... and I'd bounce
the ball two or three times, study the orange rim as if itwere,
which it was, the true level of the world, the one sure thing."

*Robert Hass*

# Tom Meschery

*Power forward for the Golden State Warriors and Seattle Sonics*

I admit sleeping in late at the Hilton,
ordering room service,
handing out big tips while other men
are opening their lunch buckets. I know
you would have scolded me:
"Что это за робота для человека?"
("What kind of work is this for a man?")
Old immigrant, I admit all of this
too late. You died before I could explain
newspapers call me a journeyman.
They write I roll up my sleeves
and go to work. They use words
like hammer and muscle to describe me.
For three straight years on the job
my nose collapsed. My knees ached,
and I could never talk myself out of less
than two injuries at a time. Father,
you would have been proud of me:
I labored in the company of large men.

## Eddie Gottlieb

*Owner and general mgr. of the old Philadelphia Warriors*

The first words he said to me were,
"You'll want to buy lots of things.
Whatever you do don't , I repeat,
don't buy anything retail. Buy
holesill, y'hear, holesill."
I heard alright. All the way
on the long drive to my first
training camp, I listened, amazed
at what I didn't know
about the game, how little
it would cost me—and how much.

## Oscar

*Oscar Robertson, Hall of Fame guard for the Cincinnati Royals*

Always at those moments
when we thought the game was ours,
out came the cavalry bugler
blowing charge. It was Cincinnati
1963, but today it's pure Hollywood,
soldiers suddenly appearing on the horizon,
the terrified Apache who always suffered
a losing season high-tailing it across the border...
Here a voice stops me and says: *But the Royals*
were only an average team. Don't you remember,
*the Warriors won most of those games.*
Not anymore. Today, I can't use
wins and losses, but Oscar's jumpers
rising over Embry's crushing picks,
the bugle's notes fading into applause—
I need those pictures, like movies
I can watch over and over.

## Wilt

A rookie in '61, I watched
Wilt score a century in one game
in Hershey, PA with the smell
of chocolate floating through the arena
and Zink's voice also in the air
*Dipper, Dipper, dunk,* announcing
each new point. That night
we all passed the ball to Wilt
the full length of the court, straight
and high into the dark around the rafters,
and every time the Dipper skyed,
he caught the ball and scored.
After the game, there was Coach McGuire,
surrounded by reporters, reminding them
he'd said before the season started,
Wilt would hit 100 points. But mostly
what I remember about that game,
is this: coach tugging at his gold cufflinks
then pointing at the Dipper as if
he'd just discovered a new constellation,
and, later, on the bus driving
through dark Amish countryside,
outside a farmer in a horse and buggy,
hurrying home in the all
too brief light of his lantern.

# Maurice Stokes

*Rochester Royal's forward, left paralyzed after an on-court accident*

*I'll not answer to coma,*
*this new name they've given me*
*without asking, as if I don't know*
*who I am. I'm Stokes.*
*I play for the Royals.*
*The game is not over.*
*I'm still in the air, the ball*
*cradled in my hand, my eyes*
*focused on the rim, fans rising*
*out of their seats, ready to applaud.*
*I've not yet made that split-second*
*decision to shoot or pass,*
*on which so much depends.*
*The moment we leave the floor*
*such calls are out of our control.*

## Tommy Heinsohn

*All Star forward for the Boston Celtics and a talented painter*

In Kansas City, in the Nelsen Gallery
I look at the famous nude of Helga
and think of Tommy Heinsohn,
his famous hook shot that curved
more beautifully than Helga's hip
and his right cross that left my eye
bleeding, and how later in the bar
below the Garden he said
he painted in the Wyeth School.
I was a rookie, and thought Wyeth
was a hotel chain. Today, I write
poems and admire the back-light
in Wyeth's painting of the dog
sunning himself in the window,
two men who made such violence
together, the work of the artist.

## Play-by-Play Men

*Chick Hearn, Marv Albert, & Bill King*

You can't out-grow those nights:
Chick, faking players high
into the popcorn stands.
The dribble-drive, shots
that never scored without
Marv's blessing, "Yessss!"
In The City, Bill King screams
"Holy, holy Toledo!"
and one more jumper aimed
from twenty feet drops
a contemptible fifteen.

Perhaps, tonight,
wherever you are stalled
in traffic in LA
or home in Brooklyn,
the radio close at hand,
and tempting, you might try
those night again, play by play
your favorite team to win.
Why not? You know their words
by heart, their cadences.
Set the dial, the true court's
left to right, drop an octave
and begin, holding one fist,
like a microphone
close to your mouth.

## Earl "The Pearl" Monroe

*In the rec leagues*
*they called me Black Jesus.*
*When I walked onto the court*
*the crowd parted like water.*
*In college, someone found a rhyme*
*and I became a pearl.*
*I guess I've been a mixed*
*metaphor ever since. Sometimes,*
*when I backed a player*
*down into the paint*
*and spun into my shot,*
*I knew before the ball left*
*my fingers it was going in.*
*At that moment*
*I could have healed lepers,*
*raised the dead.*

# Mendy

*In memory of Mendy Rudolph, one of the NBA's finest referees*

In a rain storm
from a cab I thought I saw
you on the corner, and again
I heard you make the call
against the Knicks;
a fan stood up and yelled,
"Hey, Mendy, who's
watching the newstand?"
For every fan's complaint
you slicked back your hair,
your way, I always thought,
of telling them "Up yours!"
Tonight, the wipers clean
the windshield the way
you used to wipe the air
above your head
when the buzzer beat the ball,
the losing team outraged,
refusing to believe
in your omniscience,
and the gamblers in the stands
who lost money
threatening your life.

## Jerry West

That nearly full court buzzer beater
that kept the Laker's playoff hopes alive
was never in doubt. I knew its certainty
from fingertip to rim. Jerry, as sweet
as that shot was, I want to tell you,
about another one far sweeter:
night falling and the cross-winds
of San Francisco full court pressing
All City Ray Paxton, postman
with the soft touch we depended on
in the clutch. He "called it" (something
you forgot to do) seconds before the rain
would have ended the game with nothing
resolved, summer over, the lucky players
off to college where they'd play
to big crowds indoors, safe and dry.

## Willis Reed

*Center for the New York Knicks 1977 NBA Championship team*

You limped onto the court
and made sports history. I limped
to the kitchen for a beer
feeling this pain not in my leg,
but in my heart. Only two years
out of the league and already
my body breaking down. A simple
manuever with the lawnmower,
and I heard the muscle tear. No
thanks to you, I'll probably hear
somebody at work tomorrow
say, look at Willis, only one
good wheel and able to out-play Wilt.
Horselaughs, then the bright eyes
of the dandelions staring
from the lawn, daring me to return.

## Larry Bird

For years I took for granted
your shot hitting nothing but net
believing in that old saying coaches
use about the ball having eyes.
Until one day I'd had enough
and began cheering your misses.
"Brick!" I yelled
at the TV on those rare
occasions and found I felt
relieved by your misdirection.

Perhaps that's why
waiting in lines at checkout stands
we reach for the blemishes
of our favorite stars, turn pages
to birthmarks, the crowsfeet
around the eyes of the sexy blonde,
looking for flaws we take
for granted in our own flesh.

## Magic

When you joined the Lakers
the league started counting its money.
Nike began hiring new shifts.
And the last reserve buried on the bench
saw his salary jump to a quarter mil.

I'm not jealous. Except for those times
I yell in a closed closet
surrounded by our winter clothes
until I feel better about the check
I bounced recently, the stack
of bills enlarging my desk.

Sometimes, someone asks
what I'd be worth in today's market.
I think only of bulls and bears,
those perennial rivals. Once
I answered, "the going price
for a first round draft choice,"
but knew that lie would never
reach the bottom line.

I think of your life now,
how quickly your smile
no longer sells anything,
how the Dow can rise and fall
in such a short time.

# Michael Jordan

His air curves upward
while all the rest of us,
misguided,
say we "hang."
Disconsolate and
earthbound, we know
our air merely descends.
He stays aloft,
legs splayed, tongue
a puppy flap.
Happy, so happy
three centuries later
to prove Newton wrong.

## Bill Bradley

*Rhodes Scholar and forward for the New York Knicks*

The sameness of your jumpshot
was your secret. I know
that now. Age has taught me
how repetition wears a person down.
Newspapers wrote about your habits
shooting hundreds of shots
from exactly the same places
on the court, top of the key,
freethrow line extended until
you knew those spots by heart.
I had a coach who called it
muscle memory: what you must do
to be great. Today, that dedication
wears me out.  I'd rather think
of Dick Barnett, your teammate,
who never kicked back the same
crazy jumper twice, and one time
from half court, the moment
the ball left his hand, turned
to one of those recorders of the game,
keeper of the clock and said,
"Baby, we are in oo-ver-time."

# Hakeem Olajuwon

*a.k.a Hakeem the Dream*

In Africa each morning practice starts
with warm-ups. The youngest on the team,
perhaps sixteen, always waiting for me,
sits in the thin shade below the backboard,
reading the latest article about Hakeem.
We stretch ham-strings, then slow jog
around the court. He keeps pace, all the while
talking about The Dream. "Dis donc," he says,
"With The Dream we would defeat Senegal
and be champions of West Africa.
Que pense, toi, entraineur?" What do I think?
I can't, about anything more than the red
and smoky sun rising over the opposite basket,
the heat already sweating my shirt, and how
the rains suddenly begin half way through practice.
I shag his jump shots, the ones he swears
are like Hakeem's. He says he will also attend
the University of Houston, later play for the NBA.
"Vous m'assistez?" But his shots are ugly, too flat;
they lack the back-spin, the softness of the Dream's.
I nod my head, whatever I can do, my best shot.
I am in the country of Burkina Fasso.
Its name means, land of up-right people.

# John Stockton & Carl Malone

*The guard/forward combination of the Utah Jazz.*
*Malone's nickname is the Mailman*

Stockton licks the stamp,
places it on the envelope,
and the Mailman delivers.
O wondrous metaphor
that in its wake
new car dealerships
called Stockton to Malone
are able to spring up
like wells in this arid state.

From all over Utah
the Saints will arrive
at the doors of such good deals.
This is only just.
Haven't the Lakers fallen
like the Canaanites?
Are we not in the desert
of righteousness where
a Catholic can bounce pass
on the dribble to a son of Ham
and Hosanna, score?

## Phil Jackson

*Coach of the Championship Chicago Bulls*

I finish your book, *Sacred Hoops*
and think, perhaps, you've discovered
the secret of the modern game,
that center each player can reach
with right breathing, as if the soul
were a tight muscle in need of stretching.
Team mantras, spiritual championships.

If only I'd known
I didn't have to throw that elbow
at LaRusso or stalk Chet Walker
to his locker room, spoiling for a fight
or take a swing at Wilt,
while my breathless teammates
worried for my life.
All I had to do was breathe
my way out of anger.
Lungs instead of fists.
It was that simple all along.

## Kobe Bryant

*Lakers' guard who came to the NBA directly out of high school*

Three air-balls in a row
and the face of the cock-sure
millionaire becomes the face
of Billy Harris who I told
to take the last shot
for the city championship
although he was too young,
the only sophomore on the team.
When the ball left his hand
I knew right away,
and wanted to climb the air
to pull it back before
it fell two feet short, and the fans
began to stomp their feet
and point that terrible pronoun
at him, as if you, you, you
didn't already understand
he'd never be the same person
he was the day began.
Tonight, on TV against the Jazz,
I watch you and believe
it's my fault all over again
because Billy Harris never
got his shot back no matter
what I did or said to him
for the next two seasons.

# TEACHING

## Reasons to Teach

"Why do you teach? You don't have to."
My student's last four words
a statement not a question. His voice,
the tone of average salaries in the NBA,
believing, since I played, I'm rich.

I know what he expects, that I will say
for the fun of it, or more altruistically
for the love of children, to help minds grow.

An uncle, a Texas businessman,
three years retired, come to summer visit,
at one dinner said, "Those who do, do;
those who can't, teach."
O, most unwelcome and perhaps right uncle,
should I tell this boy and now
all the other students waiting, all ears,
about near bankruptcy,
how even years later my check book
hardly balances but teeters
on the edge of money-worries.

Or should I say, poets brought me here?
Keats or Whitman, leading me by hand
to a higher purpose, to teach
rhymed or unrhymed verse
to future lawyers and veterinarians?

Or do I say I teach to write poems about money,
trying to find in me the sprung rhythm
of financial freedom, the joy
of monthly checks, automatic deductions,
the great desire to be solvent
in the sure cadence or decadence of stability?

I always wondered what the do
in "Those who do, do;" means, a verb
that by my latest count has forty-seven dictionary
possiblities, but derives from the Latin, dere,
to put, (as in: abdere, to put away.)
I like the number 4: to put forth, exert
and number 13: to create, form or bring into being,
(as in: *She does lovely oil portraits.*")

I have never put away a nest egg for a rainy day,
or CD's but had exerted myself ten years worth
in the NBA, such sweat worthy of the word, exertion.
These days I try to bring into being, the way good students
should of seeing the world clearly—not perception.
(As in: he perceives I teach because I don't have to.)

If I don't have to teach, teaching becomes an avocation
like building classic motorcycles part by part,
thought by thought, by the book or instinct, until
one day you throttle, and the engine comes to life.

Once, after a grueling week of losses,
a teammate said, "If they never paid me,
I'd still play." And my father, old immigrant,
believer in misery, could not believe
they *did* pay good money for a game, for work
you didn't hate and come home weak from drudgery.
"Sport." The word flew from his mouth like spit.

An avocation is a calling. God calls
and men and women go, without pay,
into silence, or mean neighborhoods,
or Third World countries full of malaria
to work saintly hours, grow old and die.
Why do they toil? I think of love.

Then, do I tell my students I love them?
That's why I'm here, though they're not
my flesh and blood. Still, every morning I rise
like Saint Francis and bless their essays,
usage, compound and complex sentences.

Or, perhaps, I say I teach to replace
the blind touch of ball, the space
between my finger and the rim, or worse,
what someone in anger told me once,
"You need the fans you lost."

Last year our district raised salaries three percent,
six-tenths of one percent of monthly minimum
earned in the NBA. I should plan a comeback,
get in shape, but my knees ache even as I stand here
at the podium caught between too many truths
to be truthful. "Tomorrow." I say, "you will finish 'Beowulf'
and the passage from John Gardner's *Grendel*."

## Cause and Effect

We lean forward in our seats stunned
by the pictures of our students' brains
spinning into different colors on the screen.
When normal: reds, blues, greens.
But dark, odd shapes form between the norms,
wider for every year they use cocaine,
worse than any shade of black I've ever seen.

Out from the dark stage, the doctor's
sad voice explains the consequences:
how finally blocked synapses
dull the senses, dulling even sex,
not to mention softer pleasures like steaks
or sunsets. But I cannot forget
his opening words: *Beware, they'll never*
*learn to understand cause and effect.*

Where does it show us that on the scan?
In which of the dark holes did cause reside?
Effect? So many different shapes to choose from.
I settle on the ones that look like wombs.

## Suicide

One teacher says she saw it coming
which drives the rest of us by lunch
crazy with guilt, remembering the old
ed. movie *Cipher in the Snow.*

So we promise ourselves, next period
we'll embrace all our students, even
the wall-eyed one who lurks in the back
drawing obscenities on his desk.

Of course we don't, returning to decorum
with the bell, to Marilyn passing notes,
Harry's runny nose, Carrie's menstrual cramps,
essays overdue, forgotten texts.

In sixth period, one girl by the window starts
to weep, but when I ask was he her friend,
she shakes her head; she never knew him,
but thinks he was her brother's best friend's cousin.

By then, her tears have started a chain reaction.
All around the room, students are crying
the way one can't help humming a certain tune,
or when frightened in the dark, whistling.

## Sonnet for a Future Beautician

Lord, give this little girl what she wants.
Her dream is so modest: that hair
will be beautiful and perfectly styled:
that she will possess the knack, the light touch
by which all strands will bend to her command,
sweep back or lightly fall over one eye;
that she can also manicure on the side,
hold her customers' hands gently
in and out of a cleansing liquid,
listening to their stories while she files
and decorates, cutting back the cuticles.
For this little girl, Lord, let hair
be heavenly set and on those slender nails,
allow pale half moons to rise forever.

## Film 1A

Even in handcuffs, he can't stop
yelling directions, pan left,
pan right to his son who dutifully
shoulder mounts the camera,
a machine bigger than his head,
and following that shrill command
pans to a close-up of the cop's badge,
then aims at the principal's sad eyes.
The custodian, the one who pinned
his father to the floor, hides his face.
No one cast him for this role.
I stand in my classroom door
ignoring the code that clears the halls
watching this father and son scene
being shot, worse than any B movie
I've ever seen. Later, my students say,
"Cheesy," as I try to explain the boy
crying as they haul his father off to jail,
the camera falling to the floor.

# Class of '98

As if Ben Jonson buried standing up
in Westminister Abbey—Ben in dire poverty,
too poor to buy a square greater than three feet,

will matter much when their first lover leaves
or their first child sickens and dies.
Then, what good will knowing ocean waves

made poets dream of octaves and sestets? That volta
means the wave breaks back, the way the sonnet breaks.
Still, I lecture that minutiae is the key:

Smart drops to his knees on London streets
and begs each passerby to pray with him.
Just let them cart him off to bedlam!

What's reality, I ask them. Smart wrote
his best poems a raving lunatic.
But they are only months from graduation

and, raw in the private places they know best,
want nothing of eighteenth century anecdotes.
They need to know what heals or doesn't?

Will their hearts break? Not as a metaphor,
but the "real deal." Is there a cure for pain?
Already they lean too heavily against their desks.

This morning at the start of class,
I don't know why, I told them they looked older.

## All We Can Do To Prevent Chaos

The linoleum's tight fit
makes a line plumb straight.
Each desk leg, each row of seven,
rests on that line, one behind the other.

One student jokingly says,"anal."
That, too, is a tight fit,
and for some a great pleasure.
It's my ass. Or hers?

These days it doesn't matter
what we do to feel better.
The world in such chaos, who
would blame us for a little retention,

for such slight compulsive behavior?
Who do we harm? Call it love.
Call it obsessive. Do it daily
as long as it's consentual.

## Elle

"The Perfect Summer Look" means
a blouse unbuttoned three buttons down,
the way breasts are supposed to be,
hips, thighs, if you're not five feet two
and stout, like the student farthest from my desk
who searches pages for that likeness
close to hers. She finds none,
not even one girl ordering Choux Glacés
à la Creme in the background of the photograph
of the slender model nibbling celery.
That's the hardest part, to have been
so excluded from any scene
in the lives of the beautiful people;
even if only peripherally she could be
at a corner table watching waiters,
and waitresses, all the passersby
unnaturally and gloriously slim.
It must be Paris. It must be spring.

# Trucks

Out of the morning half-light,
they come upon you suddenly
like a headache or that dog
your neighbor never leashes
that stops inches from your knee-cap,
its teeth barred and snarling.

Bumper to bumper, their grills
rise above you in the rear view
mirror: silver, emblematic,
as towerful and American
as Madison Square Garden.

That's when you wish for Guatamala
or the rain soaked roads of West Africa
after a sudden monsoon
to slow everything down, the pace
of your heart, to tropical.

That's when you pray for sixteen wheelers
stuck up to their hubs in mud,
reduced to life forever in the Third World,
without respect, like teachers going to work,
or small four-cylinder used cars.

## Student Returns to Reno High to Visit

She said "she" in answer to my question
about, as I put it, her significant other.
Now that she had graduated, I suppose
I was looking for a word that fell
somewhere between the childish boyfriend
and the more sophisticated lover.
What I deserved I got, that unexpected
pronoun—for being so formal, or
for being so obviously heterosexual.

Once my son called long distance worried
over some different feelings, and I remember
saying I'd felt the same myself in high school.
Maybe I had. Maybe walking down the hall
another young man, slim hipped,
with wide, black eyes, brushed by me,
and I felt an urge to embrace him
for our own sweet sameness?

Defiantly, that's how she said "she"
as if I'd never heard of such a thing,
teacher, male, six feet seven inches tall.
I said, "Bring her around next time
so I can see if she's good enough for you."
A silly response, but I meant it
and for a brief moment I felt
the wind our shoulders made,
that other boy and I, as we passed
each other in the empty hall,
me too young and frightened
to turn and see if he looked back.

# Weeds—Teaching Poetry at Wittenburg Juvenile Hall

None go nameless: little shit-head,
long neck, ouch! for the tiny thorns
along their stems. If I know them:
dandelion (poor cousin of the flower),
crabgrass, oxalis, their persistent roots
impossible to find and dig out
even in the soft spring earth, to kill before
they, as gardeners like to say, take over—
take over your tulips, the early crocus
and spread into midsummer columbine.

Then, you'll pay the price, bending
on your knees in the hot sun trying to find
their hiding places among gailardia,
beds of iris, mountain lupine, coreopsis.
Spurges, henbit, out to strangle your perennials.
That's when you'll forgo names except the one
these students rhyme with mother, a slant ryhme
that slants the same direction weed roots take
trying to avoid being caught and troweled.

In class when I read these lines
to them to show how poems travel
from one subject to another—the word
I use is "leaping"—some tell me
*Man, that's totally poetic.* Others look
totally worried. *So that means*
*I can go from flowers to fucking,*
*right? And what if I want to fuck*
*among the flowers, is that ok too?*

I wave off the approaching guard.
This boy, homeless at ten, rapist
and murderer by sixteen, understands
but not enough. I tell the entire class
but mostly him; yes, it's almost always
about passion. Flowers you want to touch
like breasts can't grow unless you weed first.
For a moment, the room goes silent.
It's windowless and hot. In a week
he'll be in court, tried as an adult.

# The Author

Born in Manchuria, China of Russian immigrant parents, Tom Meschery was raised in San Francisco. He graduated from St. Mary's College in 1961 and was named to the All-American team in basketball. He was drafted in the first round by the Philidelphia Warriors and played for ten years in the National Basketball Association for the Warriors and the Seattle Supersonics. After coaching in the old American Basketball Association, he attended the University of Iowa Writers Workshop, receiving his Master of Fine Arts degree in 1974. He had a brief return to coaching as an assistant coach for the Portland Trail Blazers, then moved to Truckee, California where he and his wife Joanne, a highly regarded novelist, have raised three children. Tom now teaches Advanced Placement English at Reno (NV) High School and creative writing at Sierra College.

## Colophon

Designed and printed by Robert E. Blesse at the
Black Rock Press, University of Nevada, Reno Library.
The type is ITC Stone Serif designed by Sumner Stone.
Thanks to Bill Stobb for all his help.
Printed and bound by
Sheridan Books, Ann Arbor, Michigan.